JUST DON'T STOP

MY RECIPE

AGAINST DEPRESSION

A guide

"The cure with the improbable"

1 edition

Brasil

Dados Internacionais de Catalogação na Publicação (CIP)
Lumos Assessoria Editorial
Bibliotecária: Priscila Pena Machado CRB-7/6971

L732 Lima, Jessica.
      My recipe against depression : a guide : "the cure with
    the improbable" / Jessica Lima. — 1st. ed. — Brasil : J.
    Lima, 2023.
      112 p. ; 21 cm.

      ISBN 978-65-00-61735-1

      1. Depressão. 2. Pessoas depressivas. 3. Vida
    espiritual – Cristianismo. 4. Confiança em Deus. 5. Cura
    pela fé. 6. Autoajuda. 7. Motivacional. I. Título.

                                        CDD23: 248.86

Jéssica Lima

SUMMARY

WELCOME

Life is full of ups and downs, and in those low moments you may find yourself entering or being there for a long time in the desperate pain known as depression. It is despised by the ignorant of life, who do not recognize the destructive power.

She is full of guilt, resentment, hurt, loneliness, hatred, revenge, despair, rejection, sadness, and pain. How can a person live with all this and not be applauded for every second of war won? I stop everything, I stand up and applaud you, because you are truly a warrior. I've been where you are, and I know the size of the pain.

I wanted to take my life because I wanted the pain to end, because I didn't want to feel alone anymore, because I didn't feel understood, because I tried to find solutions to my problems and every time, I tried to solve them, things only got worse, because I couldn't find a solution. solution, because I did not see the purpose of my existence; and listening to others criticizing, rejecting, and humiliating me made life lose its meaning.

I felt body aches, tiredness, and I did not want to do anything, not even the simplest things of everyday life, such as taking a shower.

The darkness of the room and the isolation of everything was what Every day for several months. In that dark room, on one of my many nights where I was screaming and crying, I had an encounter with someone who gave me this recipe which I will share with you today.

This recipe not only cured me of depression, it got me out of the bill hole that I had to pay. This counts from almost twenty thousand reais, and I was unemployed, without having anything to buy to eat or pay rent the house he lived in. Today, I was bothered in my heart to write this book, so I immediately started writing.

I wish from the bottom of my heart that this book reaches as many people as possible so that they, like me, have the opportunity to be healed and freed from depression.

Maybe, I'm a little like you. That's why I'm here giving you my recipe so that now it is also your recipe.

Enjoyable reading!

"THERE MORE INSIDE YOU"

When we are humiliated and rejected with a certain frequency, we may forget our true value, entering one of the greatest dilemmas of human beings: "What is my purpose on earth?

What is the meaning of life?" Seems like simple questions, but when not answered, they can even be mortal. That is why I want today bring directions here, for you find these answers for yourself.

With this concept, I invite you to be open to finding your answers in simple and close things, so close that they can be inside you.

I want to share a story with you: "Once upon a time, there was a peasant who went to neighboring forest to catch a bird to keep him captive in his house. He managed to catch an eaglet. Put them in the hen house with the chickens. He ate corn and chicken feed.

Although the eagle was the king/queen of all birds. After five years, this man received a visit from a naturalist at his home. As they strolled through the garden, the naturalist said:

– That bird is not a chicken. It is an eagle.

"Indeed," said the peasant. It is eagle.

But I raised her like a chicken. Is it over, there is no longer an eagle. turned into in chicken like the others, despite the wings almost three meters long.

No – replied the naturalist. she is and will always be an eagle. It has an eagle's heart.

This heart will one day make you soar.

"No, no," insisted the peasant. She became a chicken and will never fly like an eagle.

So, they decided to do a test. The naturalist took the eagle, raised it high and defying it said:

- Since you are indeed an eagle, since you belong to the sky and not the earth, so open your wings and fly!

The eagle landed on the arm extended from the naturalist. He looked absently around. Saw the chickens down there, pecking grains. And jumped closer to them.

The peasant commented:

- I told you, she turned into a simple chicken!

"No," insisted the naturalist again. She is an eagle. And an eagle will always be an eagle. Let us try again tomorrow.

The next day, the naturalist went up with the eagle on the roof of the house. He whispered:

- Eagle, since you are an eagle, spread your wings and fly!

But when the eagle saw the chickens, scratching the ground, jumped up and went to next to them.

The peasant smiled and returned to the charge:

- I told you, she turned into a chicken!

"No," the naturalist replied firmly. She is an eagle; she will always have an eagle heart. Let us try it one last time. Tomorrow, I will make it fly.

The next day, the naturalist, and the peasant, they got up very early. They took the eagle, took it outside the city, away from the houses of men, on top of a mountain. The sun spring gilded the mountain peaks.

The naturalist lifted the eagle high and ordered him:

- Eagle, since you are an eagle, since you belong to the sky and not to the earth, spread your wings and fly!

The eagle looked around. trembled like if

you experience a new life. But not he flew. Then the naturalist held it firmly, right in the direction of the sun, so that your eyes could fill with sunlight and the vastness of the horizon.

At that moment, she opened her potent wings, croaked with the typical kau-kau of eagles and rose, sovereign, on itself.

And it began to fly, to fly upwards, to fly higher and higher. Fly... fly... until it merges with the blue of the sky... Story extracted from the book "The eagle and the chicken" "Leonardo Boff."

I want to invite you to see me as this naturalist who came here today to tell you that you are an eagle.

The long years of slavery, the pain of everything that happened and is happening, and the many people who passed and still will in your life made you think you were a chicken. I want you to bring the possibility of seeing the sun so that your eyes are filled with light.

And I know that the fear of the new can

come, but allow yourself to visualize the new, the improbable, the new life, in this way, you will bring out its true origin and live your true purpose here on Earth.

"Only those who be-
lieve in the impossible,
live the impossible"

THE IMPOSSIBLE

"And behold, a woman who was for twelve years he had had an issue of blood, and coming up behind him, he touched the hem of his garment, because said to himself: If I only touch his garment, I will be made whole. And Jesus, turning and seeing her, he said, "Take heart, daughter, your faith saved. And immediately the woman was made whole."

Matthew 9:20-22

How can a woman firmly believe in something to the point of facing a crowd in their sick state with the thought, "If I just touch his garment, will I be healed?" Good, when we decide to believe in something, what the other says and even the situations around become small in the face of the desire for the reality that we decide to believe.

"I tried 99 times and failed, but in the hundredth attempt I made it, never give up on your goals even if they seem impossible, the next attempt may be the victor."

Albert Einstein

We often prove to believe, but we give up along the journey. This makes the next attempt more difficult, because the thought is: "I'm going to fail again, why try?". However, this is the key that can change your life. "Therefore, submit yourselves to God. Resist the devil, and he will flee from you."

James 4:7

Resist is the key!

Thomas Edison, one of mankind's greatest inventors, believed he could accomplish the impossible at that time: the lamp. There were several attempts, several failures, several people saying that he would not make it, for him to give up. Try something while others throw it in the face your failure is not an easy task, but not trying and living life like a chicken, knowing it's an eagle, sure is worse.

"The courage to be true to yourself even frees you from the prison of denial. When we deny who we are and our history, we deny ourselves, however, the worst denial that becomes almost incurable and that we can receive is what we do with ourselves!"

Excerpt from my book *"The power you have, and nobody told you."*

"Knowing and accepting my roots, my origin, me makes it possible to understand who I am"

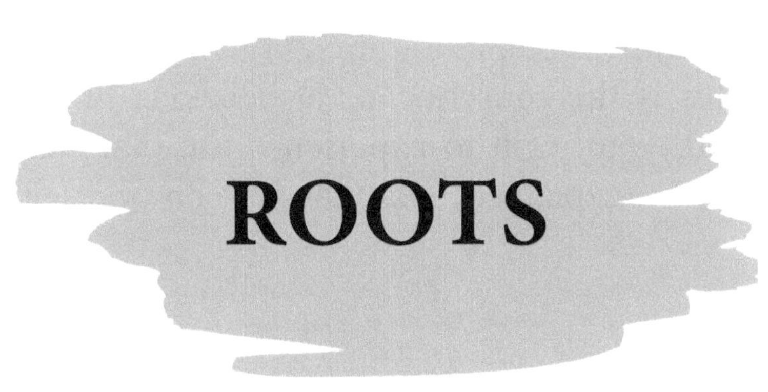

ROOTS

Then God said, "Let us make man in our image, in our likeness. dominate him over the fish of the sea, over the birds of the heaven, over the great beasts of all earth and over all the little animals – that move close to the ground." Created God man in his image, in the image of God created him; male and female he created them.

Genesis 1:26-27

What is easiest for you to believe: in its origin based on an evolution of an animal or a perfect creation of a being that can prove its existence to you through supernatural events in your life? I chose to believe in what for many is still impossible, and in the act of allowing myself, I was able to experience the impossible, and I am still living it today. This is the consequence of believing in this God, you begin to experience the that cannot be explained, but that is seen and felt.

"When pain dominates us, we become slaves to it."

In a time when the child was born first would receive the blessing of his father, who would make him the most prosperous and honorable among all other brothers, there was a certain young man named Jacob. He deceived his father – who was old and not could see – passing by his older brother, named Esau, to receive the birthright blessing. His father, not knowing he was the wrong son, blessed him.

When his brother Esau found out, he was enraged and begged his father for a blessing. Isaac; his father, knowing the weight of grief, of the hatred that was generated in Esau by what Jacob did, said, "...and he will serve his brother.

"(...) When, however, he manages to free

himself, he will shake off that yoke from his neck."

Genesis 27:40

The yoke represents that piece of wood that unites two animals to carry a load. The yoke unites two people, it is also known as soul ties. The Esau's hatred was so great that he plotted to kill Jacob, which caused Jacob to flee. Hate and hurt make us live trapped in person who did us harm, makes us slaves of that person, preventing even to achieve our dreams and goals, because we are serving the person, we hurt us. Release forgiveness to those who wounding is not easy, mainly due to the lack of knowledge of what it means to forgive.

See the four wrong thoughts of forgive-ness described in my book ***"The power you have, and nobody told you."***

"1. Forgive and forget. No, the act of forgiving will not make you have amnesia and forget what they did to you!

2. Forgiving is bringing the person who hurt me closer. No, the act of forgiving does not mean bringing the person who did you harm and who could harm you closer!

3. Forgiveness is for me to say to the person and to the world that what he did to me was meaningless. No, the act of forgiving is saying to the person and to the world that what she did to you caused you so much harm and is still hurting you, but that you cannot let that inside you, because otherwise it will end up killing you.

4. Not forgiving is a form of self-punish the other person. No, the act of not forgiving is punishing only yourself, because the other person will continue following life and often in an apparently better than yours. Thinking that she will feel bad knowing that she is the cause of her suffering and of its failure, is the greatest punishment that you can give it to yourself, not to her."

When you understand what it means to forgive, understand that the person most benefited from forgiveness is you, because it is the only way to remove the yoke that binds you to another person, it is the only way to stop being someone else's slave, it's the only way to be healed and set free.

The yoke – or soul lasso, as you prefer to call it – is also done when you don't can release forgiveness for yourself.

Soul bonds can be good, for example, the bond made between two people who choose to love and respect each other for a lifetime under the blessing of the wedding; but they can likewise be destructive. Here, in the recipe against depression, let's talk a little more about destructive. In the next chapter, I some means for you to identify them.

"How to identify a soul tie."

I will leave some examples for you:

▸ **I cannot forgive someone**

▸ **I can't forgive myself for something I did**

▸ **I can't get rid of a certain object**

▸ **I can't let go of the feeling passion for someone**

To make it clearer, I'll leave some examples of areas that generate soul ties for you to look at each of them and analyze further.

1. **Sexual area** (Related to sexual sins and illicit sexual unions)

2. **Any type of sexual abuse, physical or emotional** (Ill-resolved relationships, when you notice a deep connection between

people in the relationship); some very vivid memory in the person's memory, like a look, a touch, a situation, a sensation.

3. Exaggerated connection with some personal object or sentimental value.

4 Someone's sorrows; for whom you don't manage to release forgiveness.

5. "Personal" relationship with demonic entities.

6. A very long mourning.

These are just a few types of yokes. It is important to know that they do not come alone, they always come with sadness, bitterness and/or depression, addictions to try to block the pain or to try to escape any situation that bothers you. Some use drugs, others use alcohol, others mutilate themselves, others use sex in the most diverse ways, among others. These issues only make the situation worse, as the person becomes twice a slave: a slave to pain and to addiction.

See how much carrying the yoke only brings losses. And these are not the only losses, because they can also come: inferiority complex, psychological and physical illnesses - yes there are both psychological and physical, which are only healed through forgiveness.

A certain young woman appeared with her husband in Paul Yonggi Cho office. I was sick, given up by the doctors. She was only 30 years old, but she looked much older. Her husband said, "Pastor, I was told you could help us. That's why I brought my wife."

The pastor asked God to help him to help that woman... Then he said: "I can only help you if you tell me your story". She suddenly questioned. "Is this, by any chance, an interrogation?"

He replied: "if you continue with this posture, I will pray and ask God to reveal your past to me". And so, the girl decided to count. "Pastor, I was raised by my older sister. When I was already big, my sister was hospitalized to have a child and I stayed at home with her other children and my brother-in-law. I do not know what happened, but he and I got sexually involved, and we met several times in hotels.

I got married, and my husband never asked about my past. I carry this guilt and I resent it". The pastor asked, "Do you want to live?" She answered: "Yes". They then talked a little and the pastor prayed with her, and she was freed from guilt. Years later, the pastor finds them, and she was completely cured of the disease that, for doctors, had no cure.

Sometimes, an internal revolt is necessary to be able to free yourself from the state of slavery.

We act as our own worst judges, we punish for mistakes committed by the lack of wisdom and maturity. When I put this recipe into practice, I understood that my childhood innocence had not been touched.

"Forgiveness Allows Healing"

The passed us by and the two followed different lives and paths but remained connected by yoke. One day, God speaks to Jacob: "It is time to return to the land of their fathers." Jacob knew from the weight of the hurt he had created in his brother's heart and that he could kill but followed God's guidance. Took his women, children and everything he had and walked towards his parents' house.

At one point, they had to go through a crossing point that allowed to cross a stream. Crossed his servants, family and animals. When he found himself alone, a man came and fought with him. When the man saw that he could not control him, touched the socket of Jacob's thigh, so that he dislocated her thigh as they struggled.

Then the man said, "Let me go, for the day dawns". But Jacob replied, "I will not let you go unless you bless". The man asked him, "What and your name?". Jacob answered him. Then the man said, "Your name will not be Jacob rather than Israel, because you have struggled with God and with men and won."

Genesis 32:22-32

What do I want to bring out of this part of the story, is: sometimes God takes you away from everything and everyone to that you stay alone and only then return your look to Him and recognize your true base, for the teachings that one day you learned or heard about, but did not allow himself to truly know God.

When I was depressed, there came a time when everyone gave up on me, and even the church people who tried to help me. I was even more alone and felt even more rejected. But believe me, that was it. moment when I truly I remembered what my mother once had taught me. At that moment, I called out to God and that was the only way I could fight with Him and say everything I felt, and I cried out for his help.

And if you are at this moment, I invite you to fight and claim your blessing.

"Breaking the Yoke | Path that looks like death"

After fighting the angel, Jacob heard that his brother was on your date with 400 men. Sometimes it seems that when we follow God's leading, we are heading down a path of death.

Jacob could have backed down and disobeyed God, but he stood firm in your walk.

When God told me to confess my lie that I carried for years, to me, it was a true path of death, because I immediately thought: "what are they going to say about me? The person will only humiliate me even more", and several other thoughts of fear.

Breaking up with a toxic relationship for someone who is emotionally dependent on the other person, it may seem a way of death; reconcile with a person who once hurt you, forgive yourself for something you believe you don't deserve forgiveness, ask forgiveness for someone who dœsn't deserve, pray for someone who hurt you, help someone who only did you harm, return to the house of your parents who hurt you, leave a place to go to another unknown - everything this might seem like a death road.

Sometimes it is some of these paths that seem like death we need to tread to receive healing and walk towards the true meaning of life, with a real purpose, being free and prosperous in the areas the enemy has entered and taken possession of by not allowing ourselves to leave the state of slavery.

"When Esau saw Jacob, he ran to meet Jacob and threw his arms around him. His neck and kissed him. And they cried."

Genesis 33:4

This neck hug represents the removal of the yoke. We see the fulfillment of the blessing which his father Isaac poured out on Esau.

"(...) one day, when you get tired, you

will free yourself from this yoke."

Genesis 27:40

45

"We must see ourselves with the eyes of God"

"For it is I who know the plans that I have for you," says the Lord, "plans to make them prosper and not to cause them harm, plans to give them hope and a future."

Jeremiah 29:11

So, I thought does that mean he don't judge me for everything I've done or that I can do and still wants to give me what I want if I ask for it. Control negative thoughts yourself is not an easy task. The long years of people and situations made me think I was a chicken.

When I allowed myself to look at the sun, get to see me; I looked harder, and I could see that He did not judge me or condemned, and that all He wanted was that I would fly in His direction and that I would live my identity. I understood that flapping my wings would take effort and make me out of the comfort zone, but I also understood that this was the only way I could be free and live what I was born to be and live.

"Know ye not that ye are the temple of God and that the Spirit of God dwells in you?"

1 Corinthians 3:16

The before Jesus came into this world, when God wanted to talk to his people, he prepared a temple and a person to listen to him and pass on to the people what he wanted to say. After of the coming, death and resurrection of Jesus, He made a new covenant with his people, said that the Comforter, the Spirit of Truth, would come to dwell in our bodies, allowing us to hear and speak with Him.

Jesus said: "Nevertheless, I tell you the truth, it is to your advantage that I go away;

because if I don't go, the Comforter won't come grandparents; but when I go, I will send it to you.

And when he comes, he will convince the world of sin and righteousness and judgment.

Of sin, because they do not believe in me.

Of righteousness, because I go to my father, and you will see me no more.

And of judgment, because the prince of this world is judged.

I still have a lot to tell you, but you cannot bear it now.

But when that Spirit of truth comes, he will guide you into all truth; why will not speak on his own, but will say whatever has heard, and he will tell you what is to come. He will glorify me because he will take what is mine and declare it to you."

John 16:7-14

With this new covenant, our bodies became the temple of the Holy Spirit, further

50

declaring the importance our physical bodies have to God. "If anyone destroys the sanctuary of God, he will destroy him; for the sanctuary of God, which you are, is holy.

1 Corinthians 3:17

Reading this biblical passage was a shock to me because the person who was trying to take my life was myself.

I found that trying to destroy the temple of God, my body, it's not just trying to take it to the coffin, but it's also when the body is put in sin, when if you dishonor your body, for sin takes us away from God, and even more so when allow yourself to hold negative thoughts coming from the most diverse reasons such as hurt, rejection, humiliation, depression and so many others, for they are like a poison for the soul and for the body, attracting the spirit of death, leading the person also to have the desire to take his own life.

Many people make the mistake of thinking that the thought of death only comes for the person who has depression and make even more mistakes in thinking that only those who attempt suicide are those with depression.

An example of this is when a person has a serious problem and does not see solutions; or so the person can have a great shame, also causing someone to have such thoughts and even carry out death attempts.

When you look at the sun, that is God, you understand your identity, which is to be a child of God.

"How to Listen to God"

God speaks in simple ways because He wants us to communicate with Him. I will quote some means for you:

- God speaks through ideas

- God speaks through feelings

- God speaks through people

- God speaks through dreams

- God speaks through signs

- God speaks through voices we hear in our minds

"How to recognize the voice of God?"

Creating intimacy with Him, just like the intimacy you generate with a person makes you distinguish his voice in the middle of a crowd, so it also works with God.

"How to Create Intimacy with God?"

Take time to get to know Him, to talk with Him. So how you need to let a person be part of your life on the day by day, allowing yourself to know about her and allowing her to hear you, that's how it works with God. He left a lot of his story in a Bible and left His spirit in our body, so that this intimacy was possible today.

When He speaks, we feel peace in our hearts, even if what He has spoken is not what we would like to hear.

"One Dream 1 Rejections and more than 20 years of yoke slavery"

One of the most beautiful stories in the Bible, to me, is the story of Joseph. I say that Joseph is me, it's you, because history has a lot to do with us in today's time. And why do I say this?

First, let us look at the birth of Joseph. He was born to a mother who was barren, God saw that the woman did not bear children and said: "I will make this woman fruitful" and the first son was Joseph.

Because he was very loved by his father from birth, he became rejected by his brothers. The first fact that we see from his story is what many have already passed or even are passing, which is the act of being rejected by someone.

Joseph first rejection was for being loved by his father. Maybe, you've already been rejected by his brothers, by someone who loves, or by someone who should support you, give you affection, protection, advice from an older brother, from a more experienced person.

Joseph was not only rejected for being a son dear to his father, as well as to your big dreams. Maybe you already have been rejected by your big dreams, for the exploits he wanted - or wants - to accomplish and the person who should have given advice and support and say words to you like "go ahead, you can go much further besides, you can do it" rejected you simply for having different thoughts.

Joseph, even in the face of all rejection, remained steadfast, upright, honest, loving his brethren, remained firm in your character in your desert called rejection. Remember I said it is in the desert that our true Character comes up? Often the desert life is the time when we find ourselves rejected by people who should to be helping us on our journey.

At many points in this story, I identified and was able to extract something that led me to the success in which I find myself. Freer from the bondage state of depression.

"Stand firm in your walk because your purpose is greater than what are you going through or will pass by!"

Joseph told his dream to his brothers, and they hated him for it.

"We were tying the sheaves of wheat in the field, when my sheaf arose and stood, and her sheaves were gathered around mine and bowed before him." His brothers said to him, "So will you reign over us? You mean that, will you rule us?" And they still hated him more, because of the dream nd what he had said. "

Genesis 37:6-8

Joseph told his dream to his father, and he scolded him for it.

"Then he had another dream and told it to his brothers: 'I had another dream, and this time the sun, moon and eleven stars bowed down before me'. When he told his father and brothers, his father rebuked him and said, 'What was that dream you had? It will be that I, your mother, and your brothers will come to bow down to the ground before you?' So, his brothers were jealous of him; the father, however, I reflected on it."

Genesis 37:9-11

Ah, when even those who love us scolding for a dream, it seems to be a pain that has no end and the desire to give up becomes greater, because the doubt, fear and insecurity of being really able to do it enters.

I always wanted to graduate at some university, when I completed my 15 years old, seeing that my father had plans to get me married, I decided to tell him that I wanted to study, and he said: choose to study or be my daughter.

I told my brothers and those who spoke up said: "you just want a slut."

It was a difficult decision, I chose to study

and leaving home at the age of 15 to sell books door to door for an institution, I was hungry, I slept on the floor, I was cold, but I never went back to live with my parents.

When I turned twenty-two, I called my dad and I asked for his help again, and he solved me help financially. So, I managed to carry out my first training. The realization of a dream often comes with barriers.

This is one of the biggest barriers that made much give up on their dreams.

That is why I'm introducing you to this book, so that you have the discernment that this barrier is not an insurmountable one, because in the same way that many gave up, many managed by the simple fact of putting their faith in God, in themselves and in their dreams.

"Now faith is the assurance of things hoped for, the conviction of things not seen."

Hebrews 11:1

How can I have this faith? this faith is conquered; you are not born with it. Is it over there it's worked and most of the time you don't have help from other people to develop that faith within you. As was the case with Joseph.

The first step to conquering it is allowing yourself to recognize your roots, your true origin.

"Consequently, faith comes from hearing the message, and the message is heard through the word of Christ."

Romans 10:17

"Nothing happens if you close"

"Behold, I stand at the door and knock; if someone hear my voice, and open the door, I will come in his house, and I will sup with him, and he with me."

Revelation 3.20

God is kind, polite. He will not come into your life if you do not allow it. He wants to be a part of every detail of your life and make you fly, recognizing your identity, but that will only happen if you allow yourself to know Him. Just get to know Him and you will know yourself.

THE PROCESS

According to the adviser of relationships, Gary Chapman, every individual is born with a specific way of identifying, receiving, and giving love. And in his book, he described them as "The five languages of love."

"Words of Affirmation: Verbal compliments and words of appreciation are powerful communicators of love. They are the best communications in the form of direct and simple expression, such as: "You look so elegant in that suit!" "You look great in that dress!" "Nobody makes these potatoes better than you!"

Quality of time: When I say "Quality of Time" I want to say that you should dedicate your entire attention, without sharing it. It does not mean sitting on the couch and watching television. When time is used this way, it's the TV stations that get the attention, not the spouse. What I want to say is something like sitting on the couch with the television off, looking at each other and talking, in the process of mutual dedication...

Receiving Gifts: A gift is something you can hold onto his hands and say, "He thought of me!" or "She remembered me!" ...

Ways of serving: These ways can be as varied as possible, such as preparing a good meal, setting a well-arranged table, washing the dishes, vacuuming, tidying the dresser, cleaning the comb, taking the hair out of the sink, removing the white spots on the mirror (those caused by toothpaste), remove insects car window, take out the trash, change the baby's diaper, paint the room, vacuum the shelf, keep the car in good working order, clean the garage, cut the grass, remove weeds from the garden, remove dead leaves, vacuum the blinds, take the dog for a walk, feed the cat, change the water in the aquarium — all forms of service. so that they are carried out it is necessary to think, plan and execute (expenditure of strength and energy). If done in the right and positive spirit, it is undeniable expressions of love.

Physical touch: Physical touch is also a powerful communication vehicle for conveying marital love. Holding hands, kissing, hugging, and having sex are always to communicate emotional love to your spouse.

"The five languages of love" Gary Chapman is a book aimed at couples, but that has great meaning in other types of relationships, such as, for example: parents, children, friends etc.

Trying to show love through of a certain language that is not the person's is like trying to communicate with a person in Portuguese when that person speaks only English.

Joseph father, to show his love, gave him a beautiful tunic, and this made his brothers hate and envy him more.

HUMILIATION

One day, the father asked Joseph to see how his brothers and the flock, for they had gone out to pasture. The brothers, seeing from afar, said: "here comes the dreamer" and plotted against his life.

Maybe you've also heard someone tell you that and have even gone through or are going through the situation of seeing your brothers or people who should protect and support you plotting against your life.

Joseph was humiliated, thrown into a dry well and sold into slavery for those who were part of his family.

There in Egypt, a slave of Potiphar, among a people that were not his, GOD was with him.

"The Lord was with Joseph, so that he prospered and started residence in the house of his Egyptian master. When he realized that the Lord was with him and that he made him prosper in everything he did, he was pleased with Joseph and made him administrator of your assets. Potiphar left his house in his care and entrusted him with everything he owned. Since he left him in charge of his house and all his belongings, the Lord blessed the Egyptian's house because of Joseph. The blessing of the Lord was on all that Potiphar had, both in the house and in the field."

Genesis 39:2-5

Have you ever been in the situation of doing the right thing, what was right, and others plotting that you did what was wrong, even though you knew the truth? It was what Potiphar's wife did, and that lie sent Joseph to prison.

He could have been murmuring against God, "I'm doing everything right and now this." But no, he stood firm in his character, knowing that God was in control of everything.

"But the Lord was with him and treated him kindly, giving him the friendliness of the jailer. So, the jailer put Joseph in charge of all those who were in prison, and he became responsible for everything that happened there."

Genesis 39:21-22

And there, a slave, imprisoned, he continued to exercise his calling to serve God and the people. Joseph was a great administrator and trained his skills using them in Potiphar's house and in prison. "Every branch that, being in me, does not bear fruit, he takes away; and every one that bears fruit he prunes, that it may bear more fruit."

John 15:2

Joseph was pruned, and maybe, you are being pruned!

Sometimes, some bad things happen in our life, not to bring us down, but to prune us towards something bigger.

Other times, it is just because we're in

this world of sin that isn't our home. But God said that he would return and that he would take us from this Earth (John 14), and he said even more: "And God will wipe away from his

eyes all tears; and there shall be no more death, nor mourning, nor outcry, nor pain; for the first things are passed away."

Apocalypse 21:4

Many times I felt like I didn't belong in this world and only here I realized that I really don't belong; we are here passing through, because one day our Father will bring us back close to Him, and the only thing I need to do, while on this Earth, is to recognize my identity as a daughter and walk with Him.

I must remind you that, with or without God, bad situations can happen. The difference is: with God, you will not be alone, and you will go through situations more lightly, with wisdom and with the certainty of victory.

THE FRUIT OF HELPING SOMEBODY

Have you ever helped someone and been forgotten by that person? Joseph helped 2 Pharaoh's servants, who were jailed for displeasing him by interpreting his dreams. The men were the chief cup bearers and chief bakers.

"The chief cup bearer, however, did not remember Joseph; on the contrary, he forgot about him."

Genesis 40:23

God tells us to do it without expecting anything in return, but so does He. says he does not forget his children.

Everyone can forget about you, but God never forgot or will forget you!

"Can a woman forget of the sucking child,

so that she does not have compassion on the son of her womb? But even if she were to forget him, I will not forget you."

Isaiah 49:15

"Everything has its time, and there is time for every purpose under heaven."

Ecclesiastes 3:1

Two years later, God made the chief cup bearer remember Joseph at the exact moment when Pharaoh had a dream and could not find anyone to interpret it.

"God honored the faithfulness of Joseph."

After he interpreted Pharaoh's dream, God used him to place Joseph as the second most powerful man in all of Egypt; and Joseph managed Egypt, but before, managed Pharaoh's house as a slave, then managed the prison as a prisoner slave.

POSSIBILITY OF REVENGE

Years later, Joseph finds his brothers, who were going to buy food in the only place possible to do so, because God had sent a man to interpret Pharaoh's dream and prepare the kingdom for the famine that would come. And there, seeing his brothers, he had the opportunity to get revenge for everything they had done. But he did nothing; even with anger within, he kept himself blameless, just, kind and loving to his own, and Joseph, decision was to forgive his brothers.

So be you a Joseph! Remain firm in your path, being principled, honest, fair, and compassionate even if with the one who is rejecting you, because our essence tells us to do that.

One of the greatest examples we have of rejection was Jesus. He was rejected by greater authorities at the time still when he was in his mother's womb, as they wished for his death; later it was rejected, humiliated, beaten, spit on His face and killed him, even though he was upright, fair, kind, helping his neighbor with healing and deliverance and fulfilling your purpose. Until today, even after all His deeds, it is still rejected by many. Including, you may have been one of those who have already rejected it or who still reject it.

THE UNLIKELY

"But God chose the crazy things of the world to shame the wise, and chose the weak things of the world to shame the strong."

1 Corinthians 1:27

When I found out that I could be cured, the first thing that crossed my mind was: "Who am I to receive healing? I've done so many wrong things, maybe I really deserve this suffering". My guilt was so great that I wouldn't allow myself to let go of the pain, even if it destroyed my life.

I knew the story of Raabe, the prostitute, a woman who lived doing wrong things and who was humiliated and rejected by everyone for the things she did.

She had been raised in a sinful culture where people believed in gods of statues and did not believe in the God who works wonders.

One day, she was given the opportunity to be released. Immediately, she seized on this opportunity, and it made her not only be freed, but also be the one whose off-spring would be born the man named Joseph who would humanly care for the son of God, Jesus.

"You will again have compassion on us; you will tread underfoot our iniquities and cast all our sins into the depths of the sea".

Micah 7:19

God looks at the heart. If we ask for forgiveness, He not only forgives us, but He also sets us free and blesses us.

"Steps I took which led to healing of depression"

• Listened and sang gospel praises practically 24 hours a day; when I didn't sleep listening to praises, I slept following the next step, which you will see. That me helps to ward off bad thoughts and feelings of oppression. It's good to hear people that bring you hope. find someone like this on the internet, see if it has the divine principles that bring you hope and faith.

• Listen to Joyce Meyer or Helene Tannure preach. Hearing them was like a vitamin for my body and mind.

• I asked God for forgiveness for all sins.

• Whenever the feeling of being a victim came to my mind, I would say: "I am not a victim, I do not accept this spirit of victims."

• I started to thank every morning still in lying in bed. At that moment of "I have to get up, but I still have a little time".

• Whenever bad feelings about everything that happened to me surfaced, I said: "I am not a victim."

• I didn't stop with the projects of setting up my own business, even though I often went to work crying.

• I took all the things that connected the past to me and that house and threw them in the trash or gave the objects to people I knew I would never see again.

• I prayed in every corner of the house, casting out all the demons, and then I asked the angels of God to dwell in that house. Because I no longer wanted to go home, I felt that it was the worst place for me to be. When I started to pray casting out the demons, things inside the house started to fall, I saw that there was a lot of oppression inside the house and not I gave up. I turned on that praise that I most he liked it and sang, and prayed, and said: "now here dwell angels sent by God."

• I broke the Soul Ties made through of sex. I will leave it to you step by step how to do this in the activities chapter.

•I tried to help other people with something that if I did, it would help the person and not would make me feel bad for thinking I was lying to people and to myself.

•When something bad happens, I choose to think, "I know I don't. I'm alone and something good will come of it, and in time I'll know what to do; so, I will not torment myself."

• As those who were trying to help me gave up and stayed away when I went to church, I went with the feeling of, "I know that those who are there they gave up, but I know that the Lord does not have given up on me, and so I will go, go in, worship, listen, and come home to do this again in my house".

• When the feeling of loneliness came, I cried and said: "if you are with me, I can do anything, come and spend your hands on my head while I sleep."

• Release forgiveness for everyone who somehow it had hurt me every day: I said: "I release forgiveness in the spiritual world and in the physical world.

• I started to tell myself that I am not guilty, and that if I was guilty of something, I forgive myself.

• I carried old lies, so I decided to tell the truth and free myself from this burden; I called the person, told the truth and asked for forgiveness.

• I made a covenant with God.

• I started reading the Bible for at least 10 minutes every day.

• I began to bless the lives of people who somehow hurt me.

• I started to avoid contact with people who lived murmuring about life; when there was no way, I put my headphones on with the praises.

• I stopped with the soul ties, the ties that by logic I managed to get away from.

• I started walking from Monday to Friday.

• When I got better financially, I looked for someone in the field of therapy who had the divine vision and principles to listen to me.

• When I got better financially, I bought courses that would help me get even more into the other level I wanted.

• Looking at messages in the early hours of the day made me anxious so I only used my cell phone for what was necessary and preferably after the first 4 hours of my day.

• I DID NOT GIVE UP.

"He will wipe away all teardrops. There will be no more death, neither sorrow nor crying, nor pain, for the old order is passed away".

Apocalypse 21:4

JUST DO

NOT STOP

Isaiah 41:10

This is one of many promises what God does if you will just accept Him and be faithful to Him. There is nothing impossible for God. In other words, any illness you have is possible for God.

A certain man very powerful and honored by all, named Naaman, became very sick, an illness that had no cure. One day a girl, who knew it existed a man who could help, used a means so that that mighty lord would know, he heeded that message and went in search of his healing. When He arrived at the place, the person who performed the cures sent his messenger to give him the prescription of what he should do to be healed.

When he received it, he was indignant,

because what He told man to do was not within their concepts, beyond to be an improbable thing.

As Naaman returned to his home, indignant and murmuring at what the man had told him to do, his servants asked him, "If the man told you something hard to do, maybe you wouldn't do it? Do what he said." And Naaman listened to his servants and did so. While doing this, visually nothing happened, but he continued as he was instructed to do. At the end of the process of what the Man had told him to do, he was healed. This story you will find in detail in 2 Kings 5.

If this man had not listened to the girl's message and gone in search of healing, would that one have been healed?

If this man, upon receiving the message of what he should do, had ignored the message and the advice of his servants to do the improbable, would he have been healed?

If this man had given up even in the process while steadfastly carrying out the healing prescription, would that one have been healed?

I invite you to see me as that girl who used a means to tell you that there is a cure for you.

I invite you to see me as the one who sent Naaman the recipe.

I invite you to see me like those servants who advised Naaman to do the unlikely. Because nothing is impossible for God!

"If you remain in me, and my words abide in you, they will ask whatever they want, and it will be granted."

John 15:7

It is not an easy journey, but it is possible. I won and so did other people. You can win! Start by taking your first steps. Believing and having faith. "So also, faith by itself, if it is not accompanied by works, is dead."

James 2:17

Your actions must declare the healing you have declared on your lips and in your heart, for they are what reveal your faith.

"Without faith, it is impossible to please God, because whoever approaches him

97

needs to believe that he exists and that he rewards those who seek him."

Hebrews 11:6

Only those who believe in the impossible live the extraordinary. I declare boldness, faith, healing, and deliverance in your life in Jesus name.

Hug,

Jessica Lima

ACTIVITIES

I also leave some activities. Feel free to allow yourself to live the new. on my channel from YouTube (@metodomife), you will find a playlist entitled meditation; you will find in it a video with the name of "my moment". It is a suggestion of praise which you can listen to do the following activities.

Activity one

Recognizing God as my savior and his identity as a son and heir.

Say it aloud:

"... I recognize today Jesus Christ who came to this world, died for me to give me the right of salvation; I recognize and accept you as my only savior, in the name of Jesus, Amen."

Activity two

Releasing forgiveness and blessing.

Say it aloud:

"I release forgiveness and bless (... person) and everyone who one day made me bad. I release forgiveness into the physical world and spiritual and I do not allow this pain, this heartache, keep enslaving me. bless the life of everyone, in the name of Jesus, AMEN."

Activity three

Breaking Soul Ties.

Say it aloud:

"...In the name of Jesus, I repent of having made a wrong alliance with ... and now I return all the pieces of that person's soul and take back the pieces of my soul."

"...And all the others that I don't remember, but that the Lord knows, I release them from my life and return all the pieces of soul that is in me, and I take back all the pieces of my soul and in the name of Jesus. I completely withdraw from such people. I am free, I FORGIVE ME AND I FORGIVE those who hurt me, I allow myself to be free from the state of slavery and from every addiction that I submitted to for the slavery of pain that not even I knew or know, and I recognize today my identity in Christ as a son of the Lord Jesus Christ, AMEN.

Activity four

Acts that reveal my identity.

Now, when situations come up, ask yourself how Jesus would act and act like He would act.

Reveal your faith in your actions.

"Because our fight is not against people, but against the powers and authorities, against the rulers of this world of darkness, against the spiritual forces of evil in the heavenly places."

Ephesians 6:12

102

THANKS

First, I am grateful to God, because what I am, what I have and what I do comes from Him. I am grateful to my parents, because in their way, they helped me to become the woman I am today, my dear mother who constantly intercedes for my life and does not stop believing in me. I am grateful to my family and friends who supported me on my journey, especially to a friend and sister Lucileia Gomes who, even miles from distance encourages me to be better, she was an instrument of God to encourage me and to write. I am grateful to a great friend, Paolo Zanni, for believing in the value of this book and helping me on this journey, including reviewing writing in Italian. And everyone who somehow took part of this journey.

BIOGRAPHY

Jéssica Lima, Brazilian and Italian, born in Peixoto de Azevedo/MT, Brazil in 1987. Author, founder of @metodomife, Messenger of the Gospel of Peace, Speaker, Professional And Self Coaching, Emotional Intelligence, High Performance Mentality, Leader Coach, Life Coach, Behavioral Analyst, Specialist in Positive Psychology, Clinical Hypnosis, Clinical Psychoanalysis, Clinical Psychotherapy and others related.

NOTES